AF226047

This **STEM** book is designed to introduce children to a vulnerable marsupial.

There are additional facts at the back of the book to deepen your exploration of this topic.

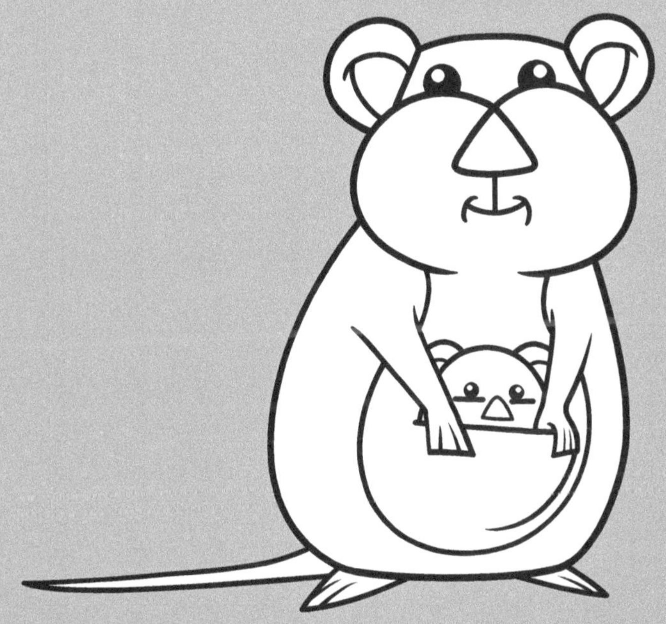

Published by CEY Press
821 Grand Ave, Suite 119
Pflugerville, TX 78660

Copyright © 2022 by Carrie Casey
My First Quokka Book

ISBN: 978-1-954885-24-0

Text copyright © 2022 by Carrie Casey
I

My First Quokka Book

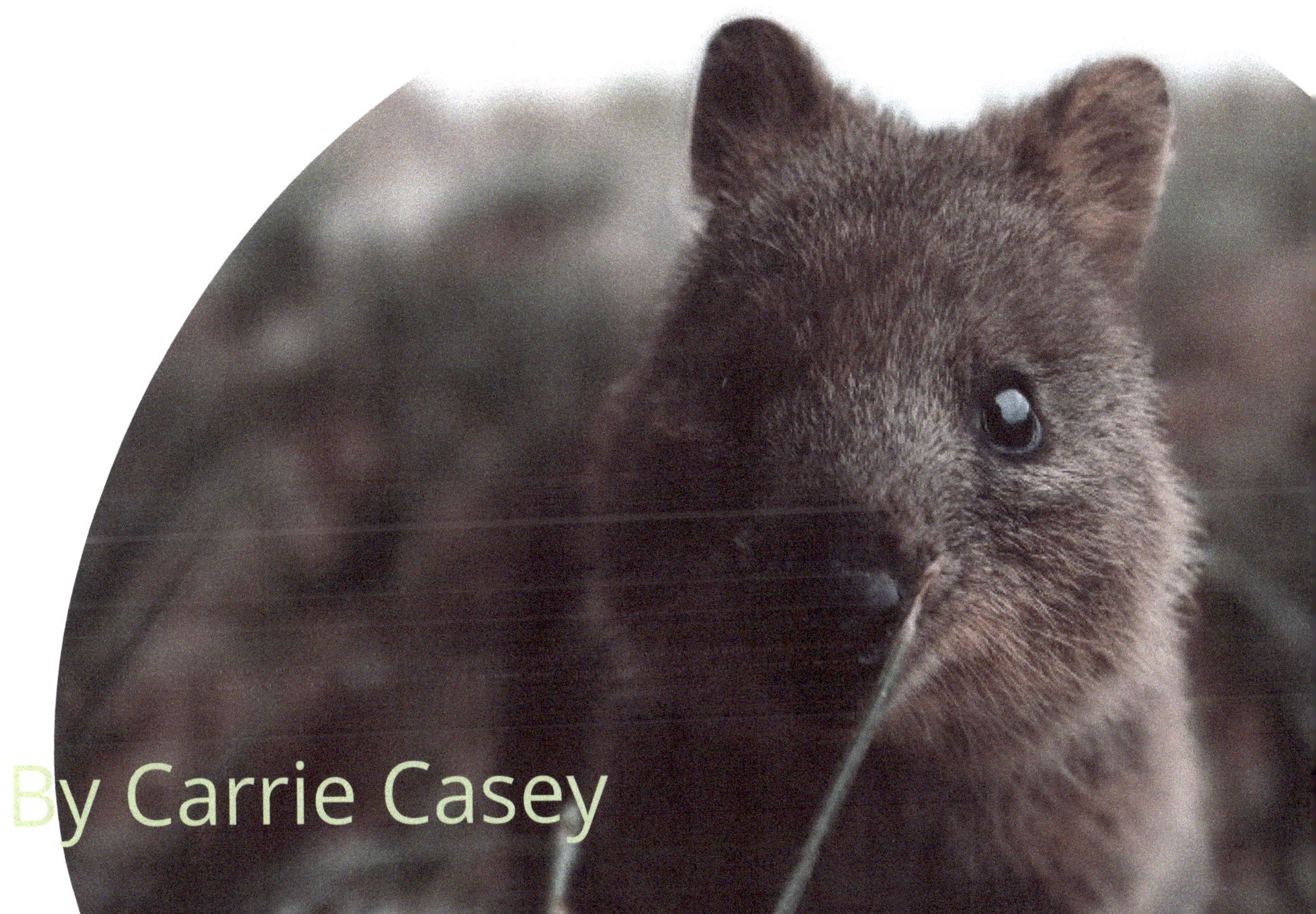

By Carrie Casey

Meet the Quokka. The happiest animal on earth.

pronounced /ˈkwäkə/ or /kwok-uh /

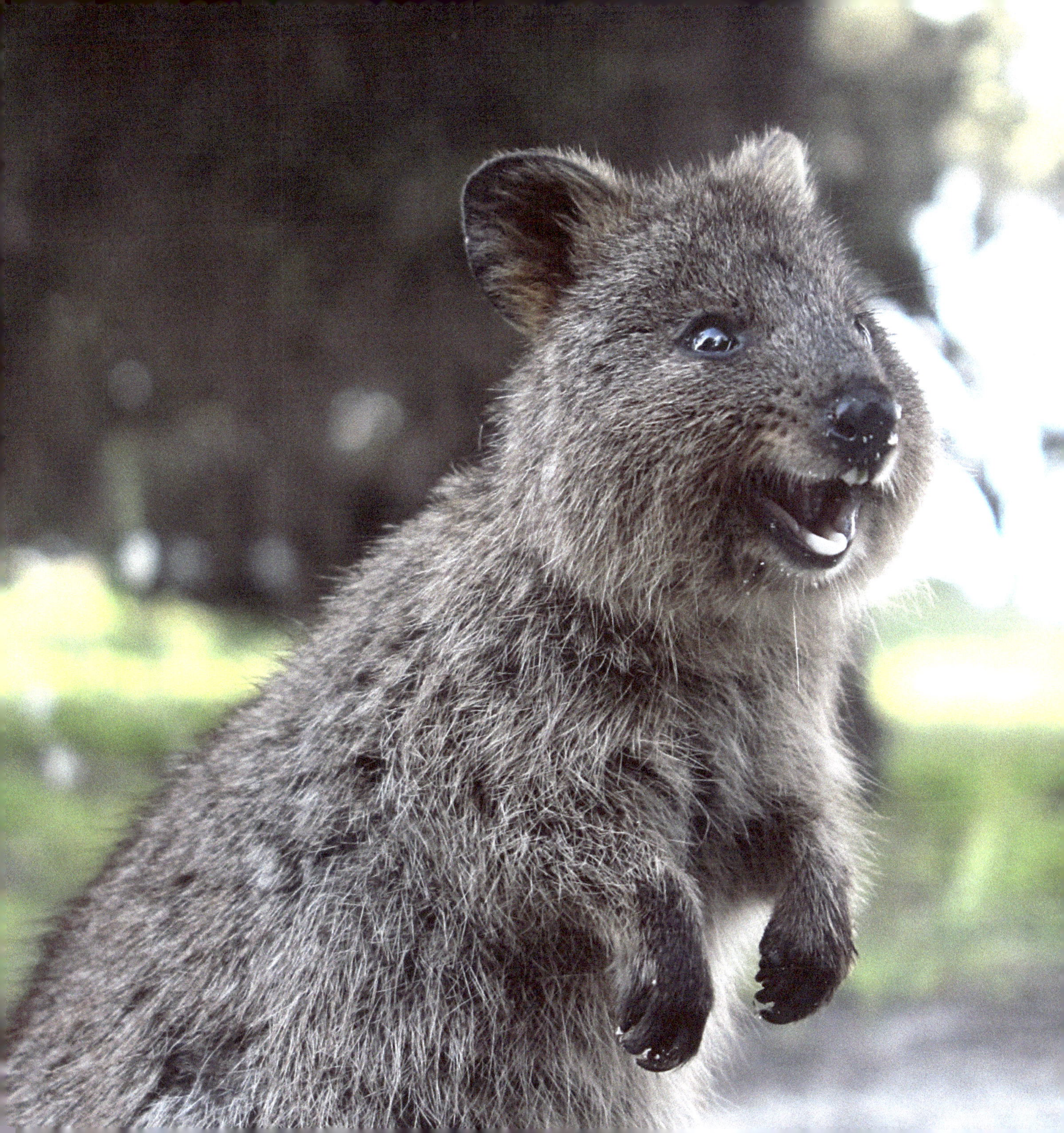

Isn't that a funny name?

QUO͞OOO KA

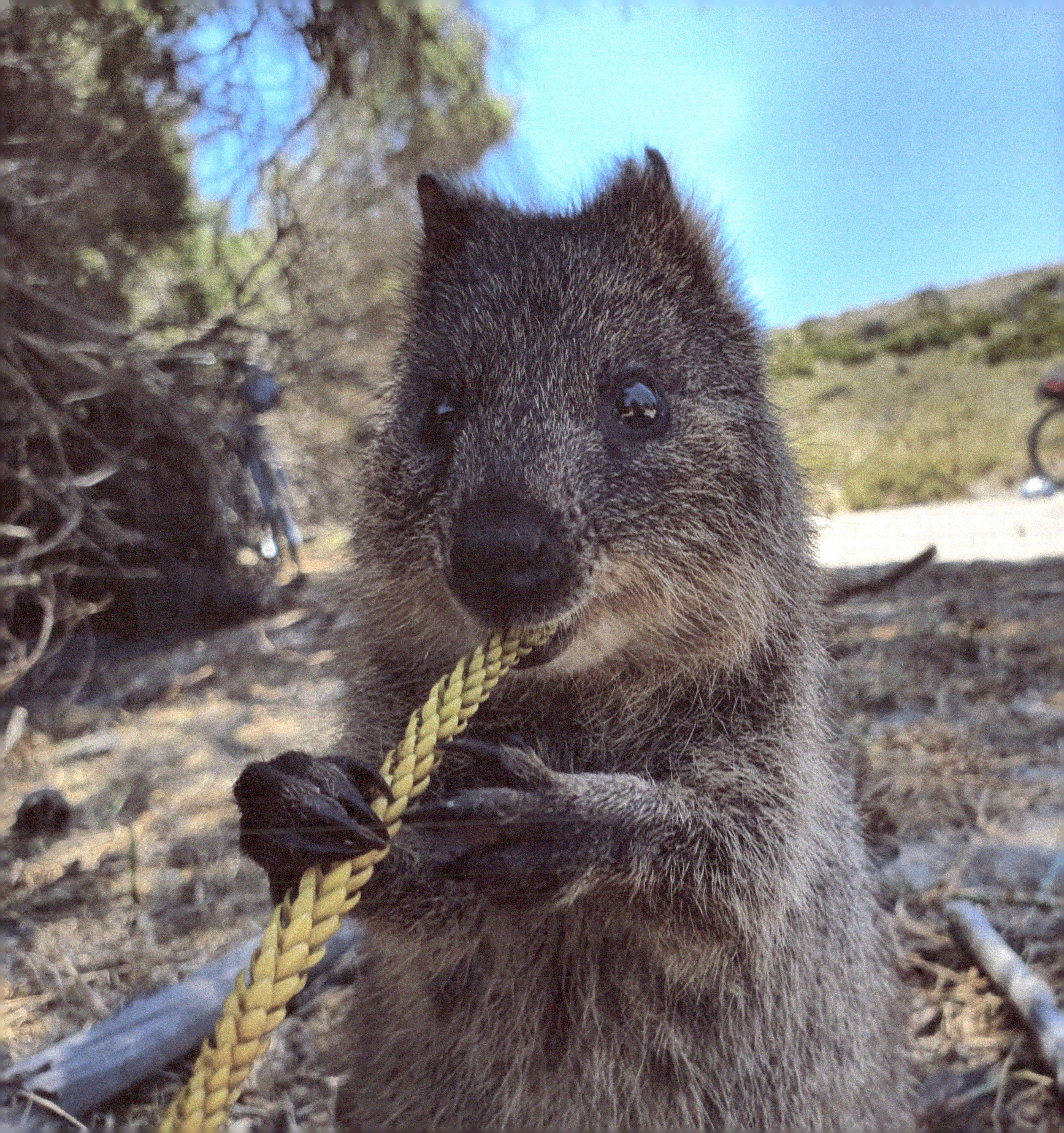

They are small,
friendly
Australian animals.

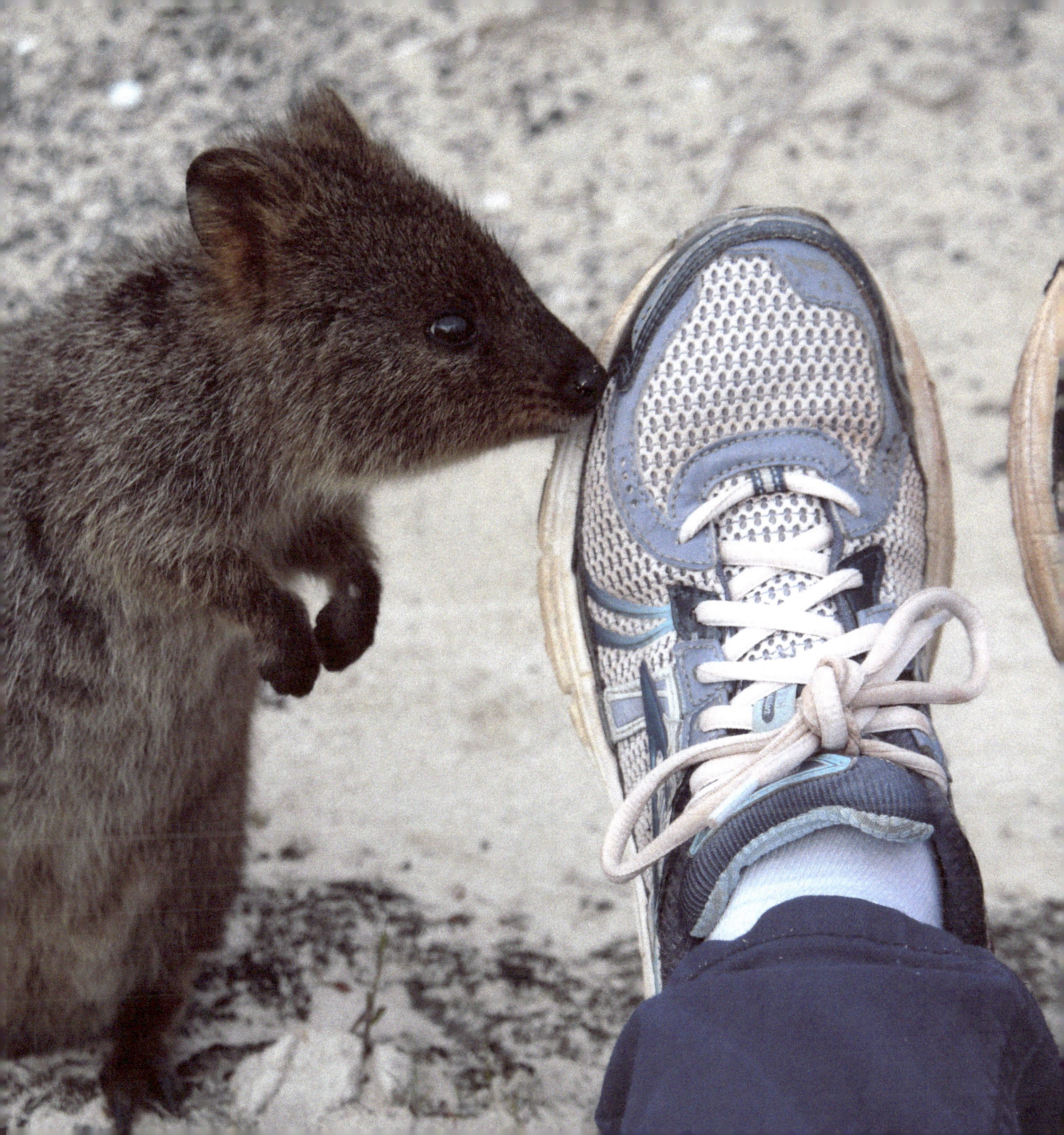

When most people think about Australia, think about Kangaroos.

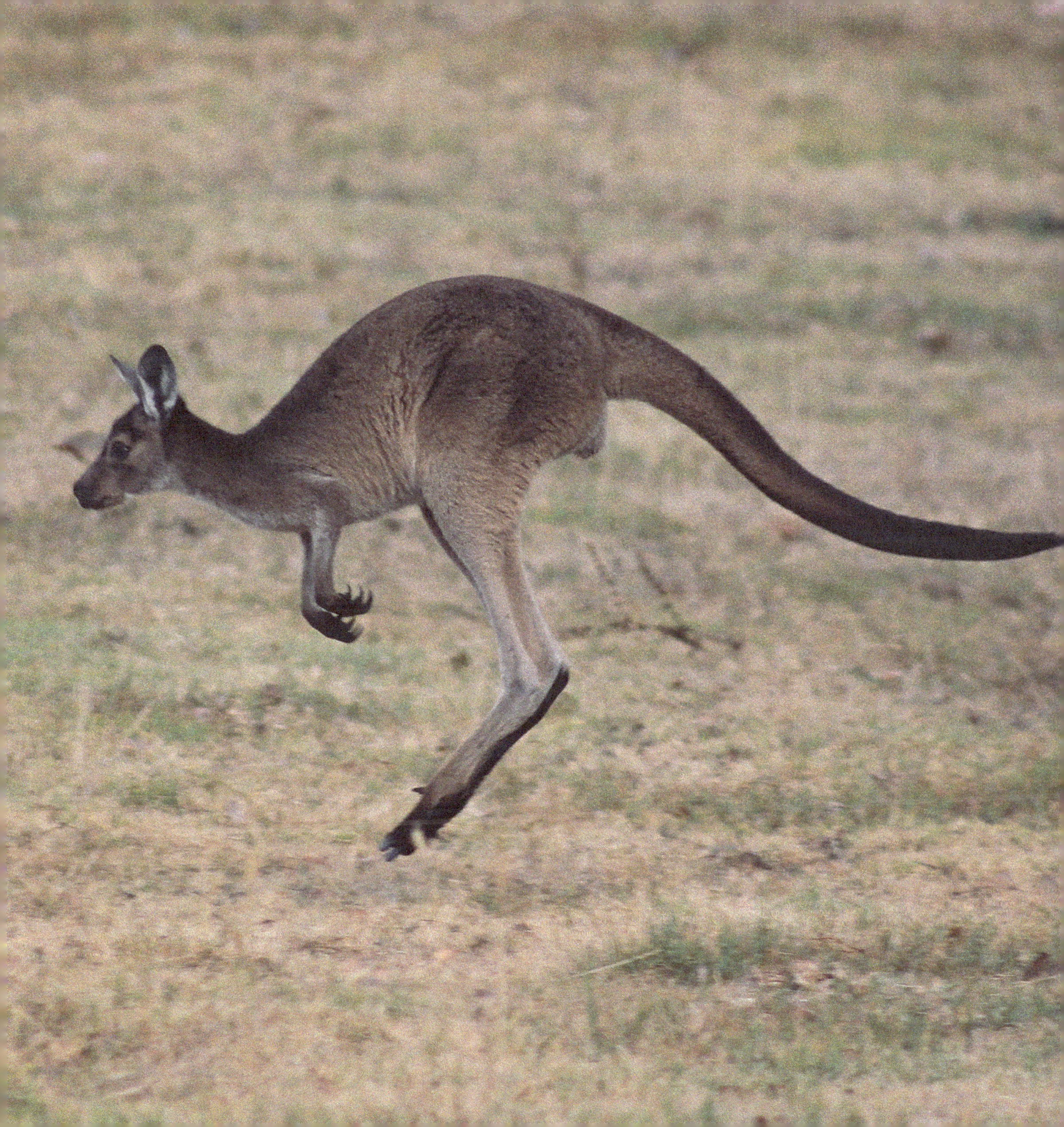

Kangaroos are Quokka's bigger, more famous cousins.

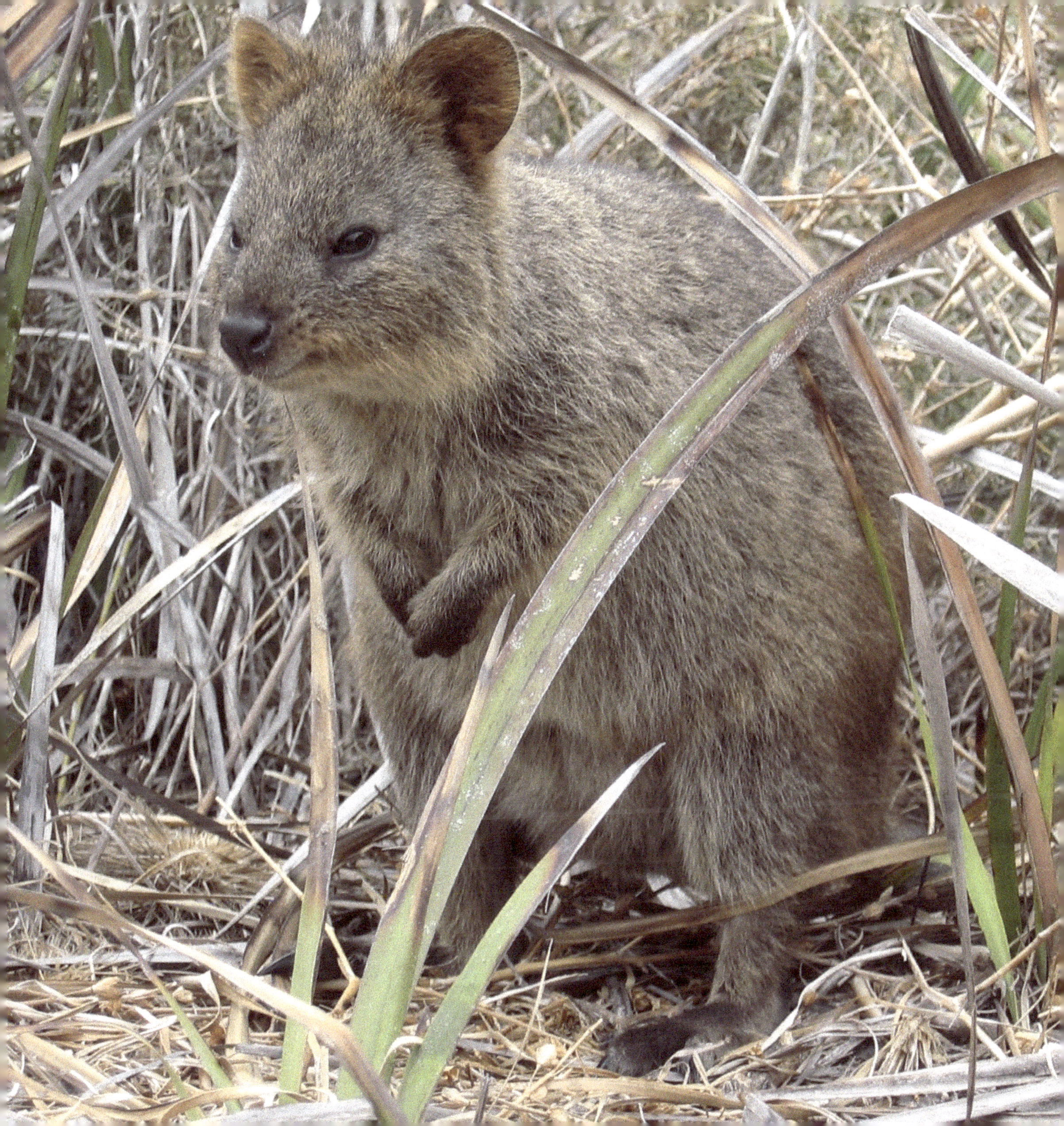

Quokka moms have pouches for their babies like kangaroos.

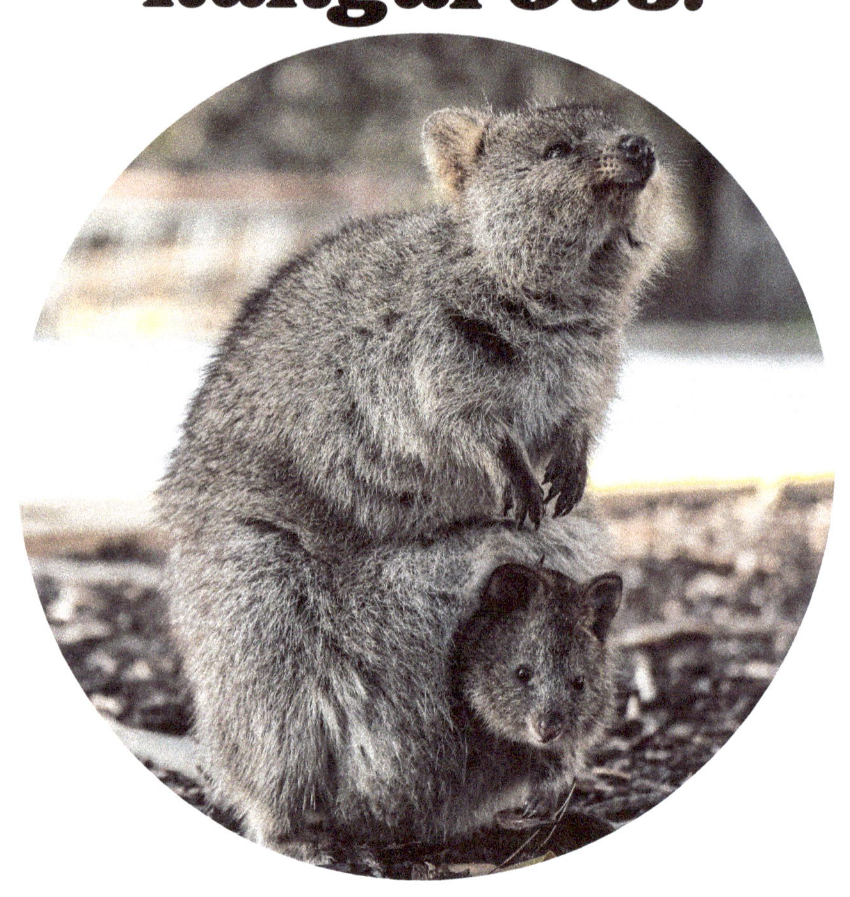

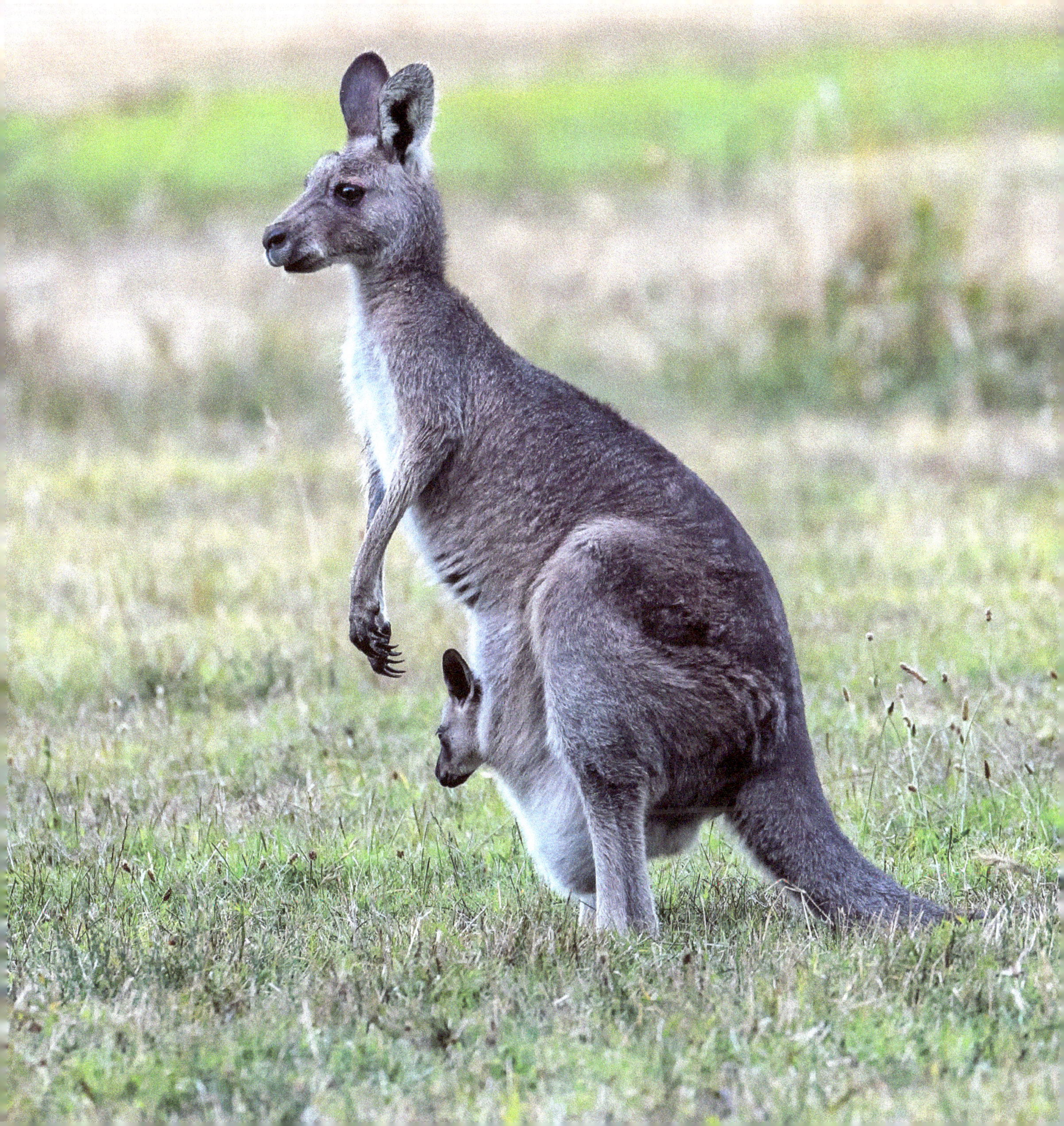

The Quokka babies
stay with their
mothers until they
are grown up.

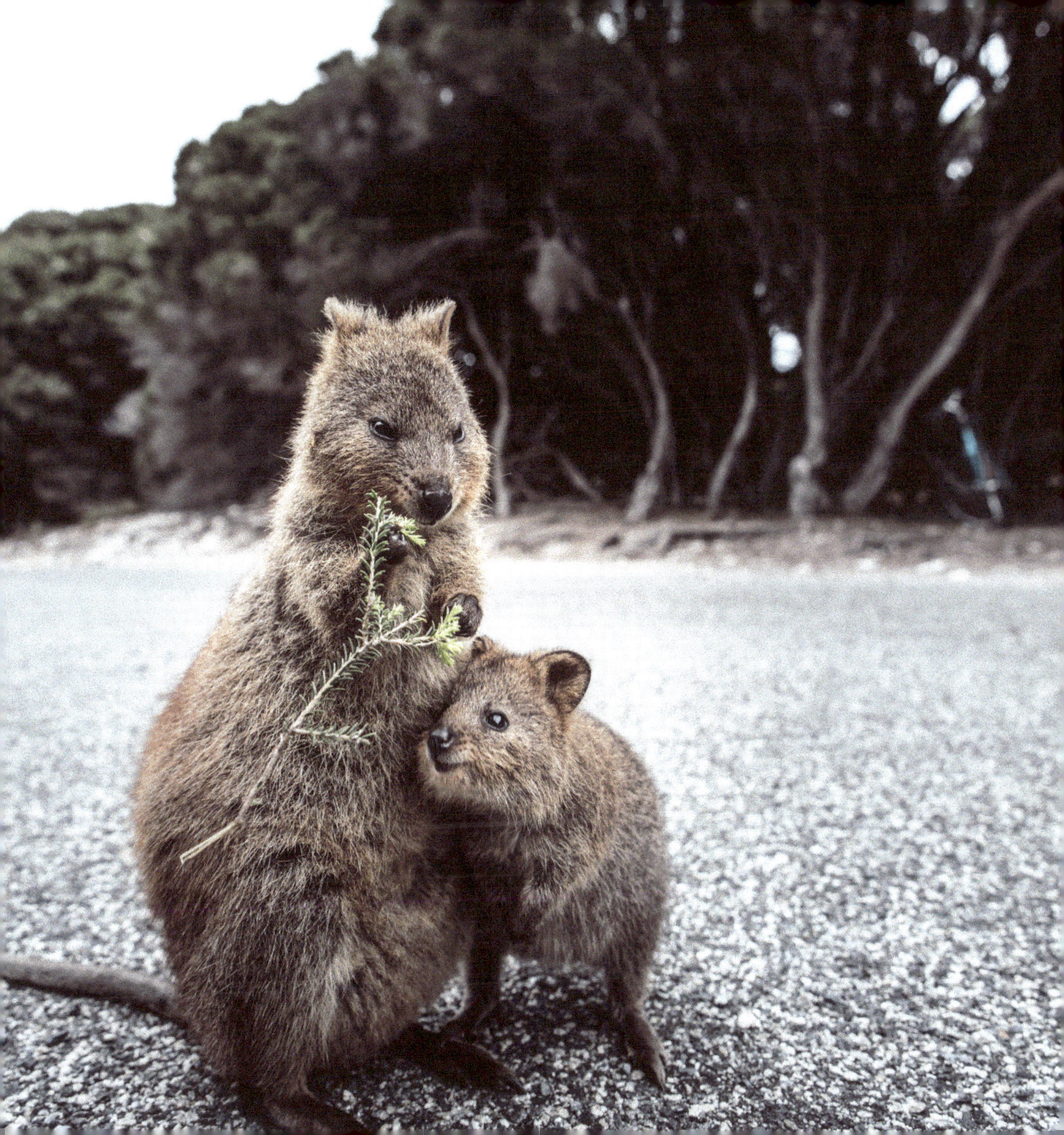

This Quokka mom is sharing her food with her child.

(Called a joey.)

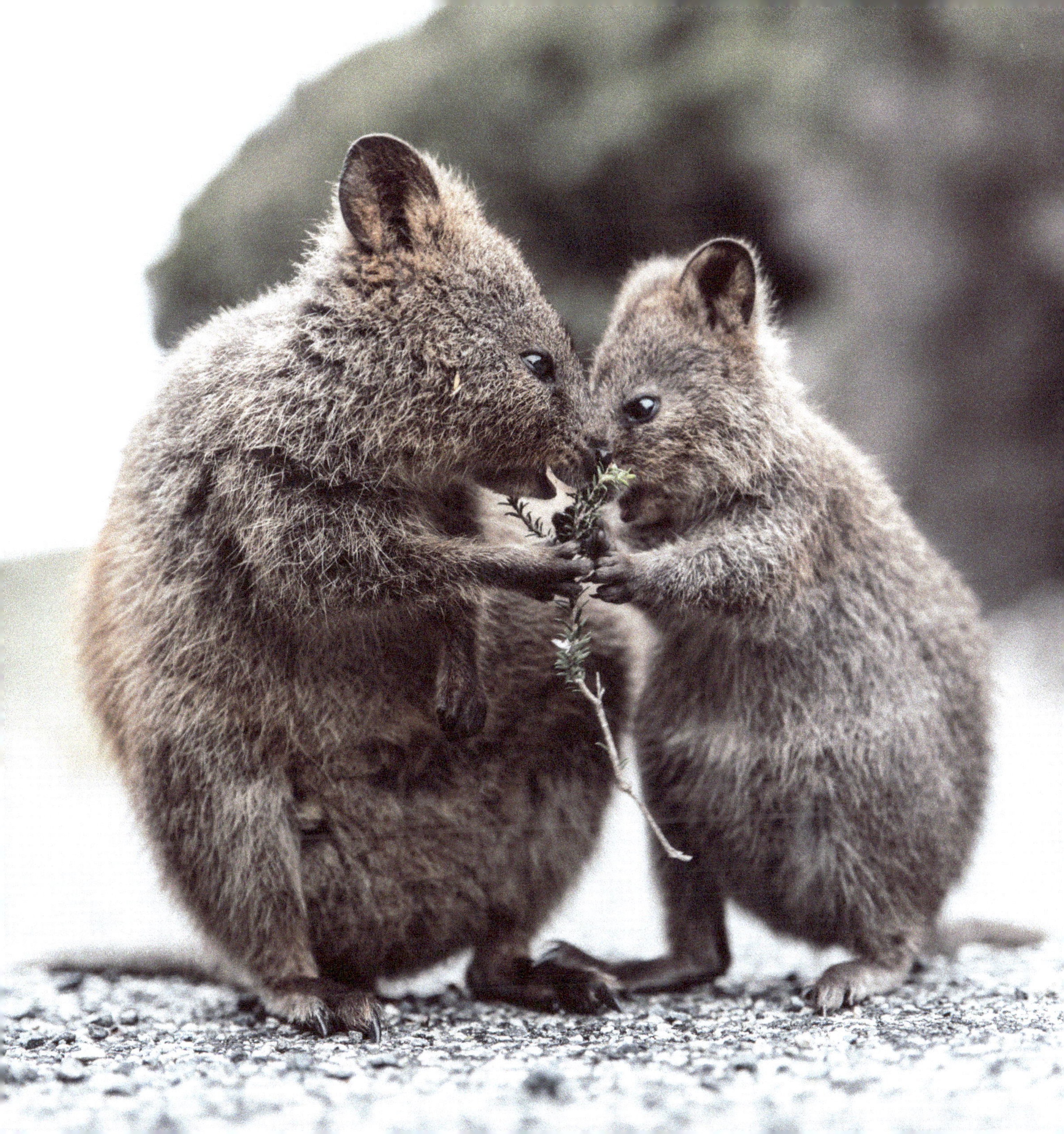

Quokkas have a happy smiling face & small round ears.

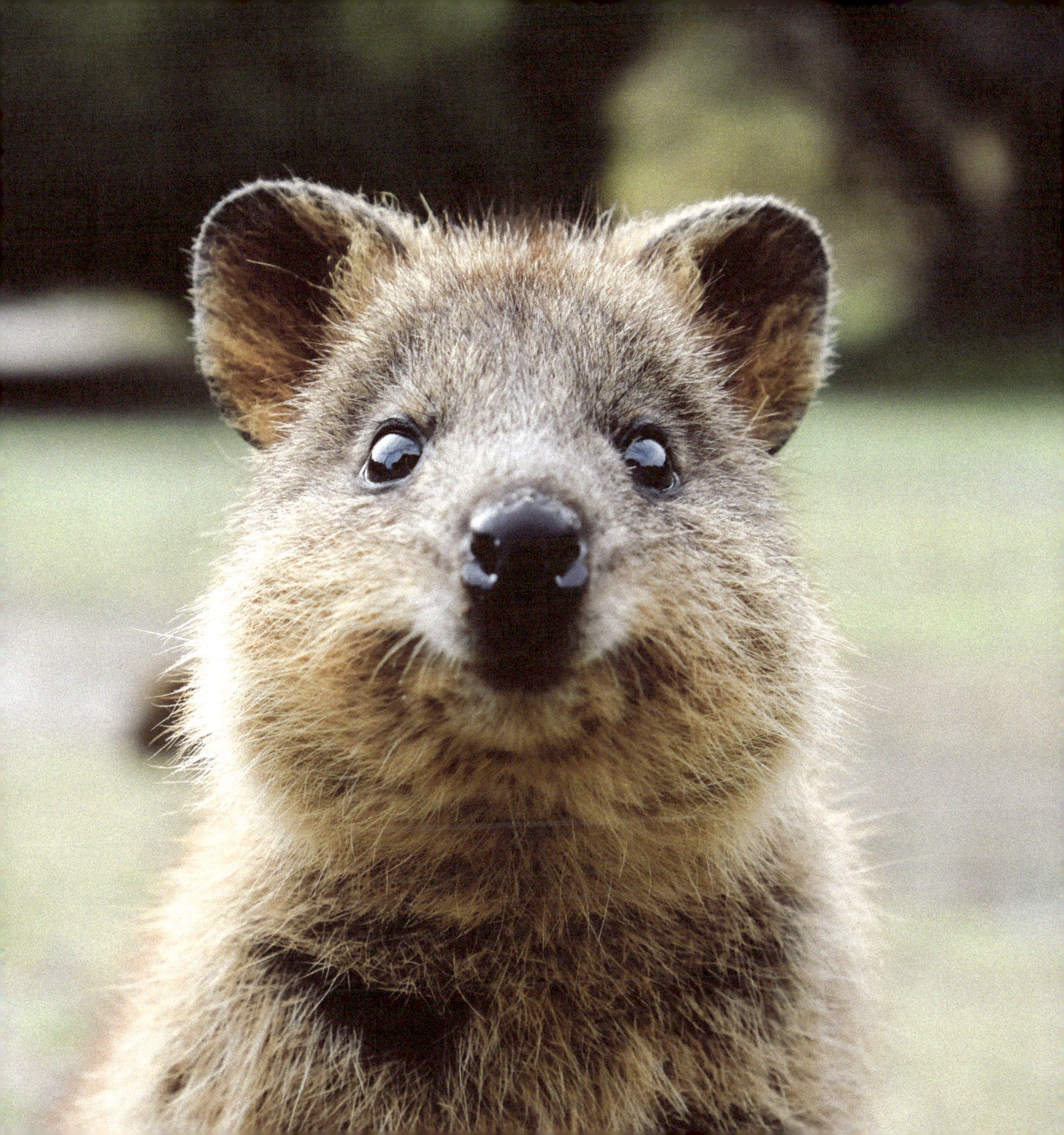

That smile brings lots of people to where most of them live.

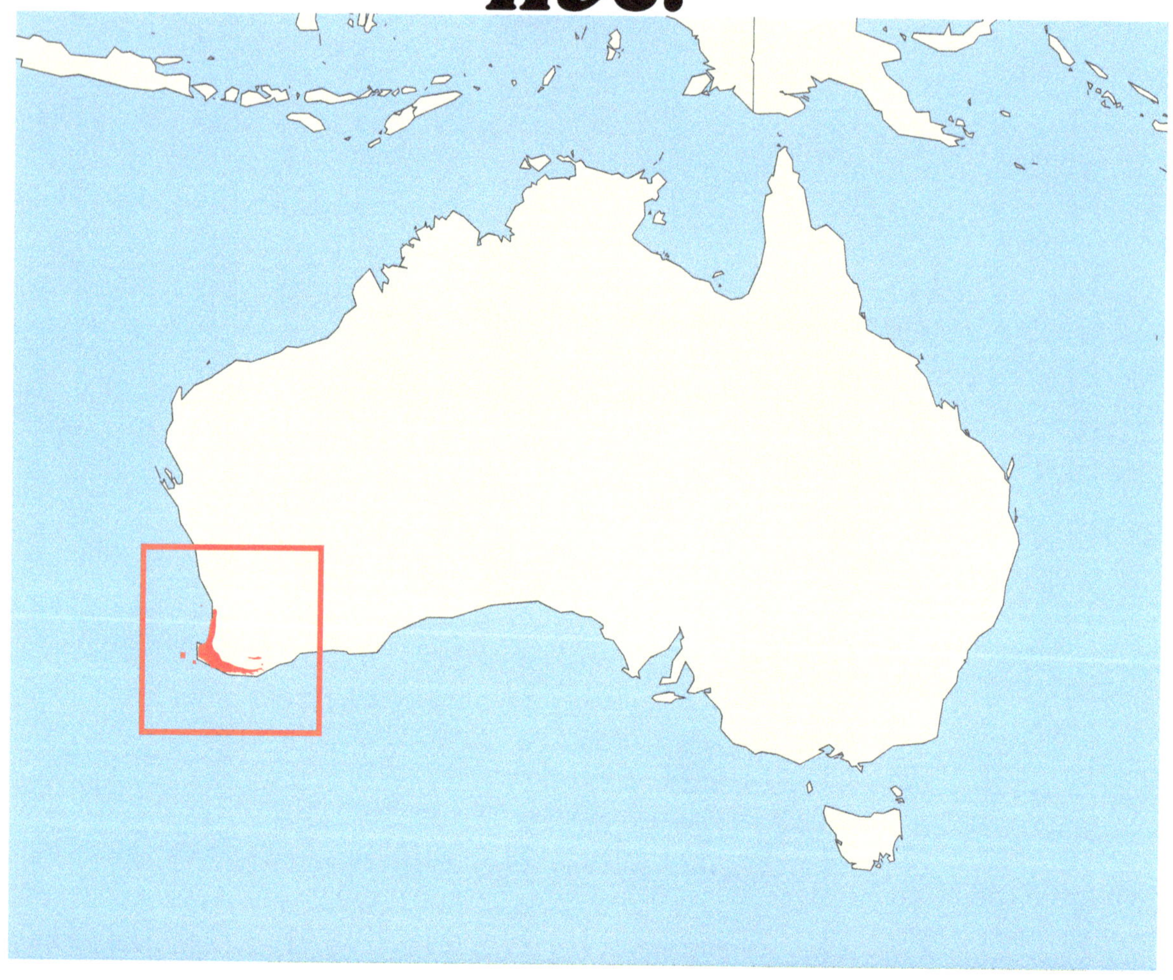

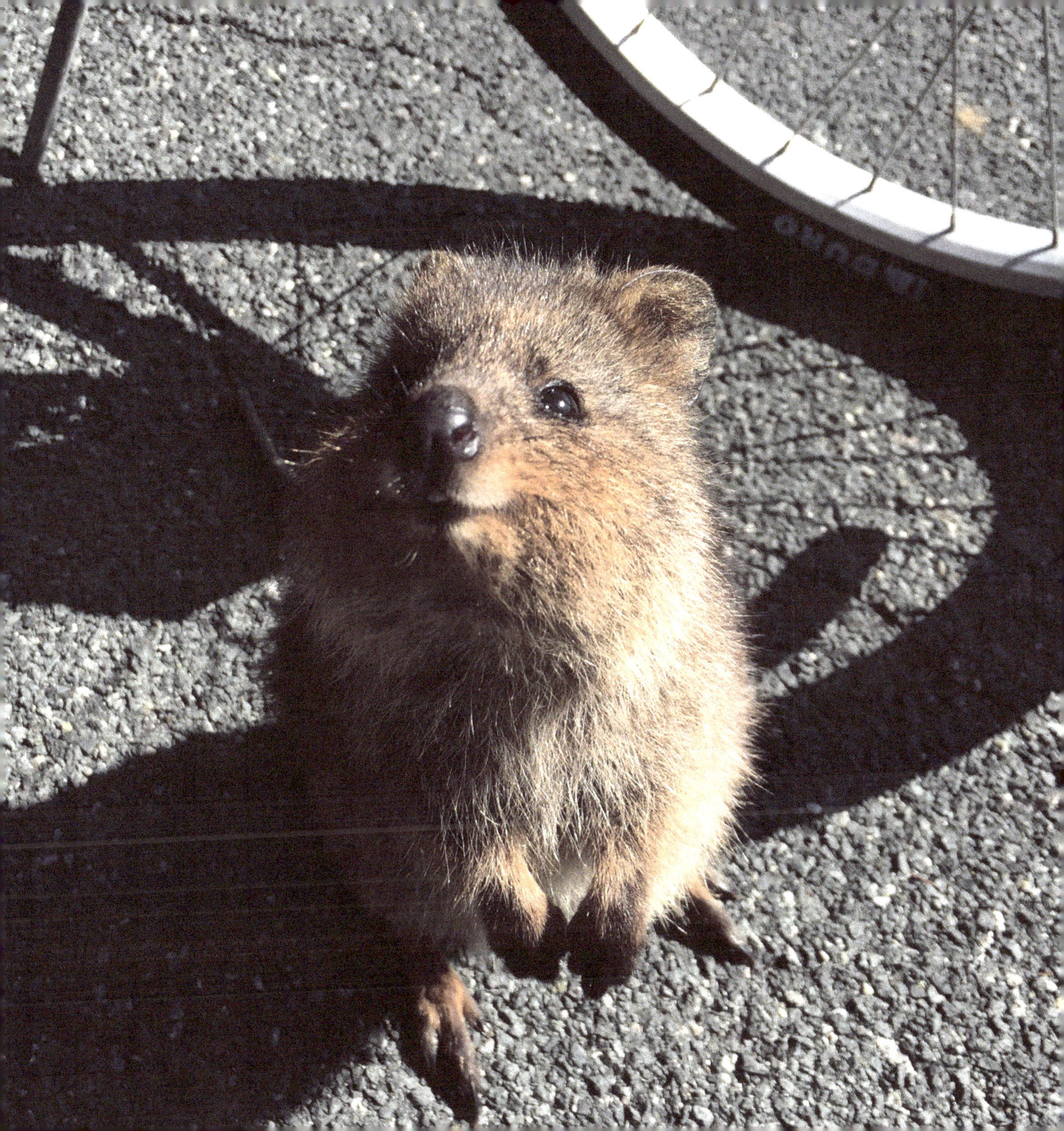

IMPORO

They spend some time on the beach.

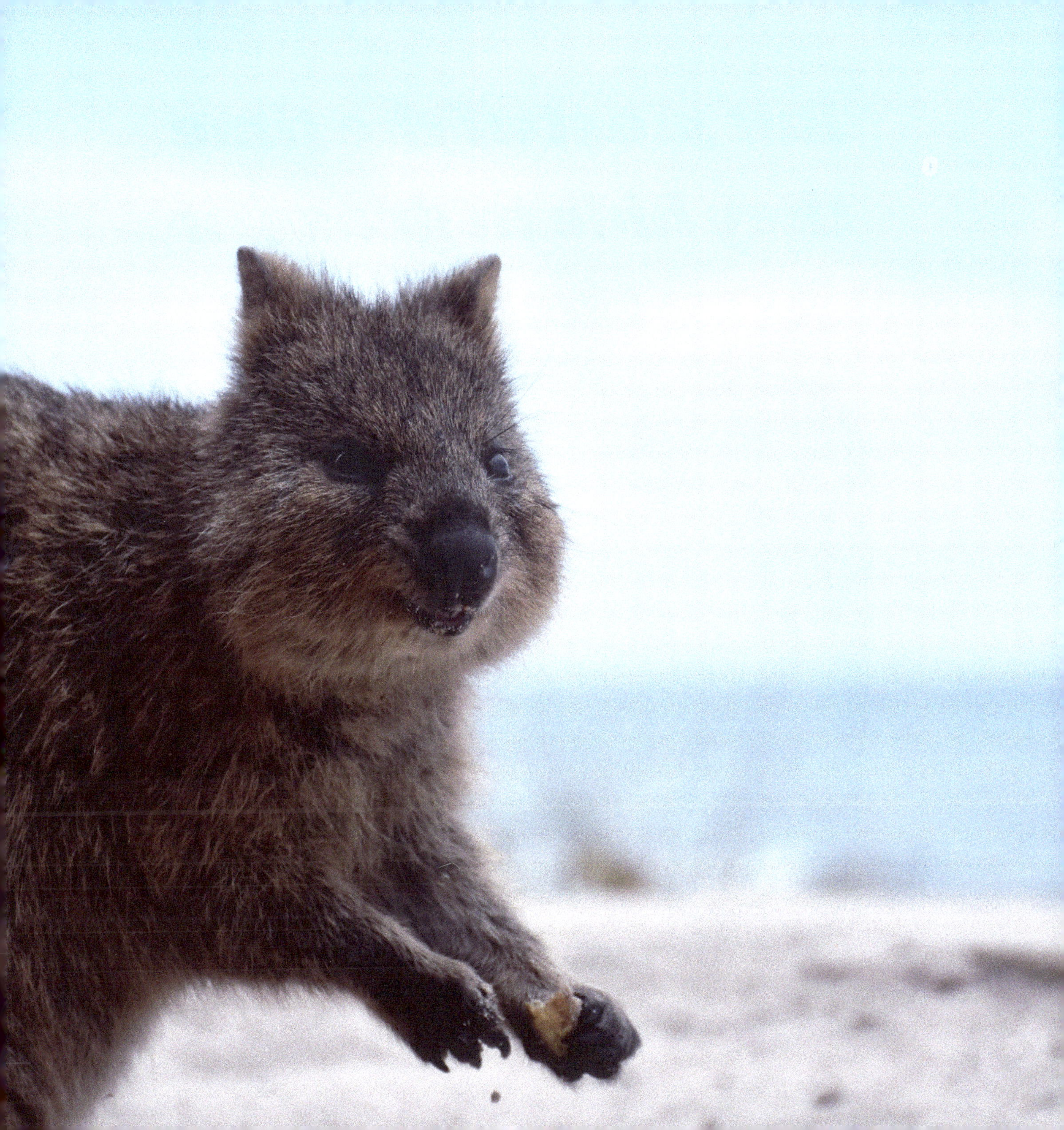

But most of the time they hide in grass or bushes.

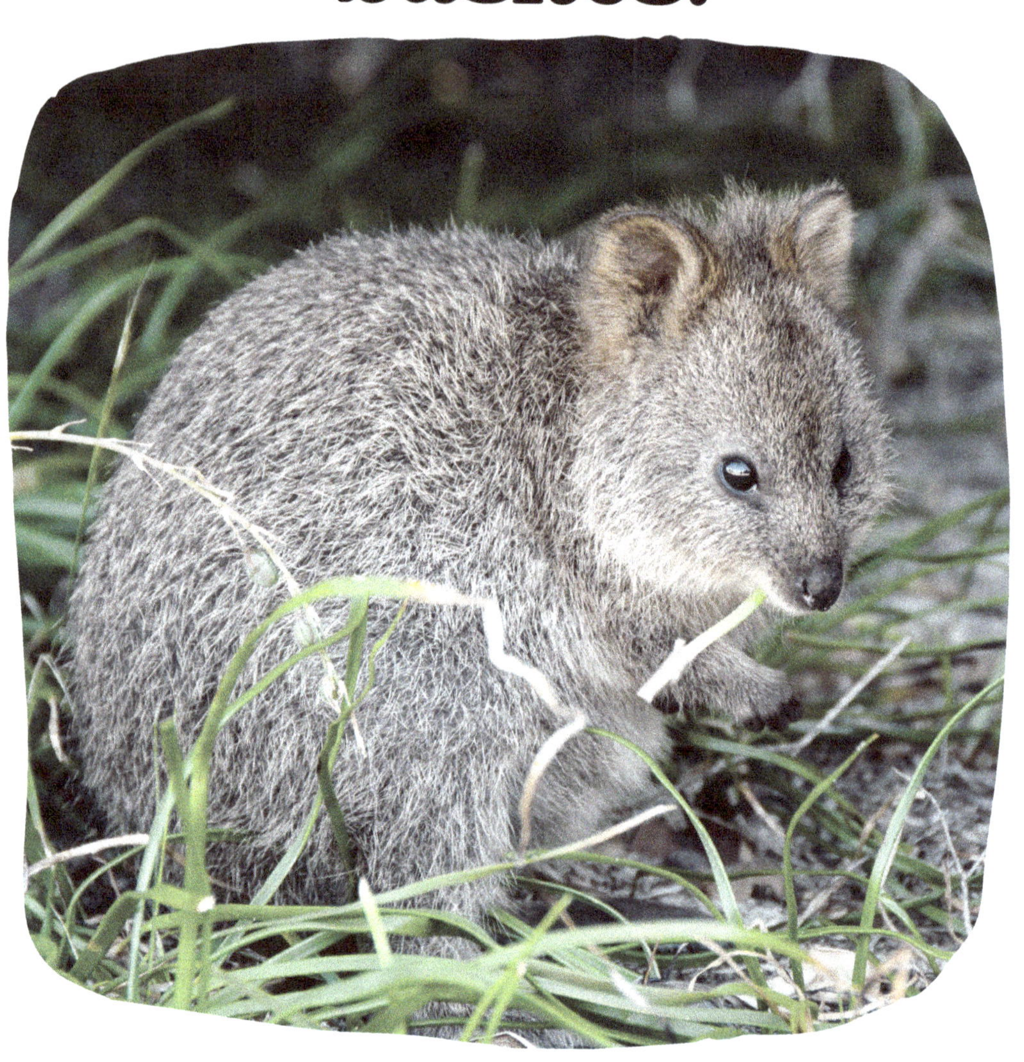

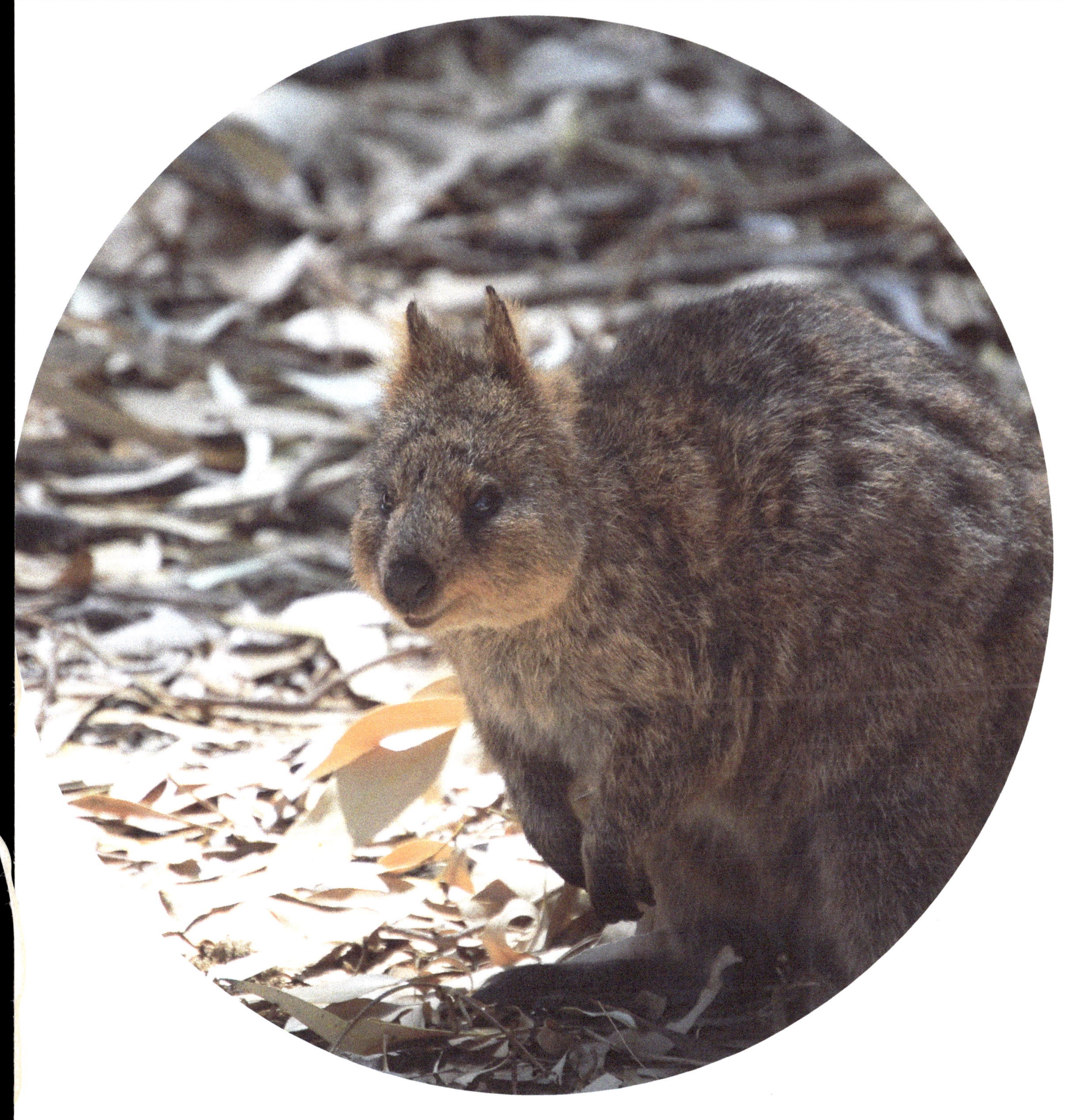

They find their food of grass, berries and leaves away from the beach.

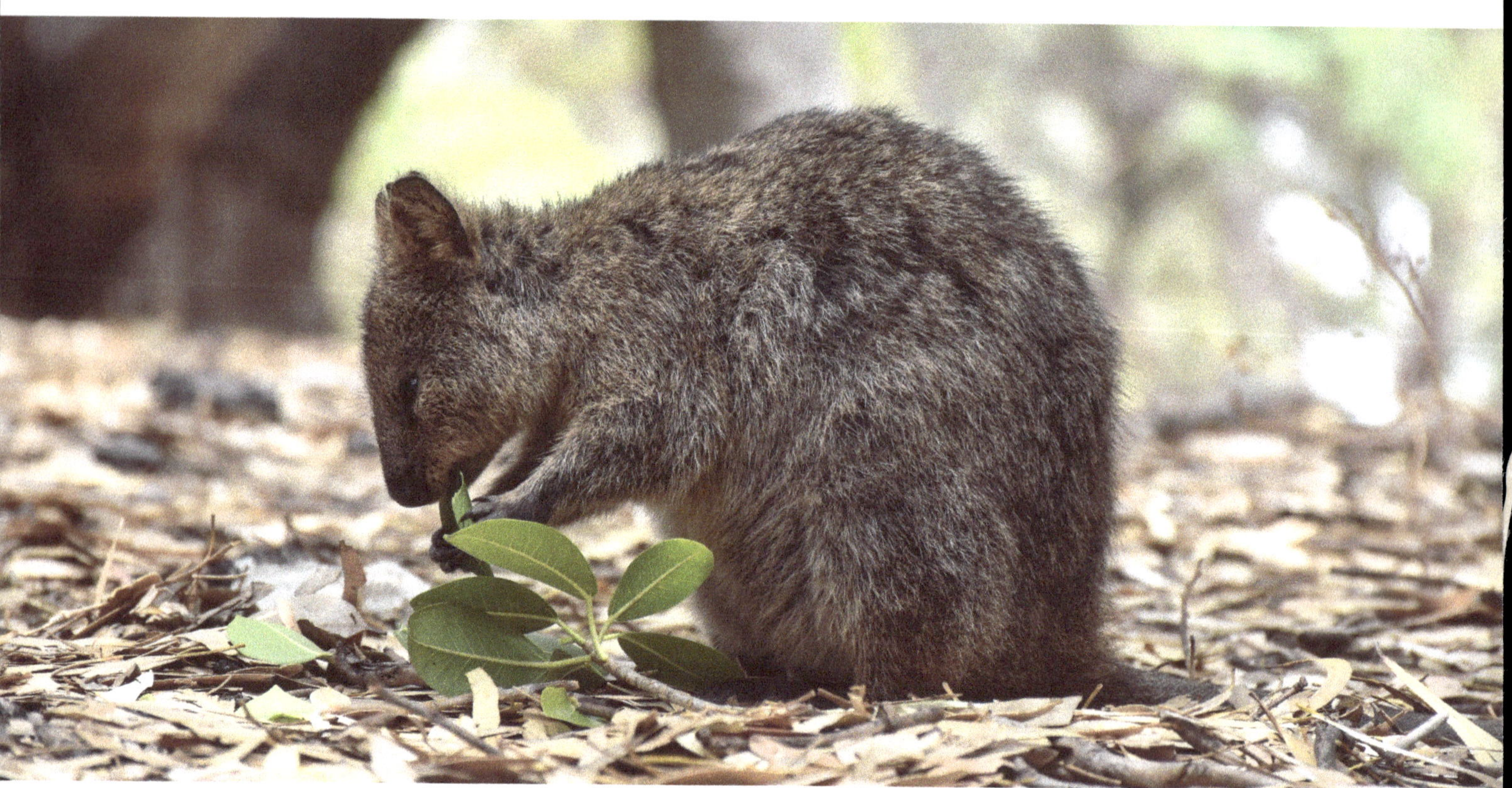

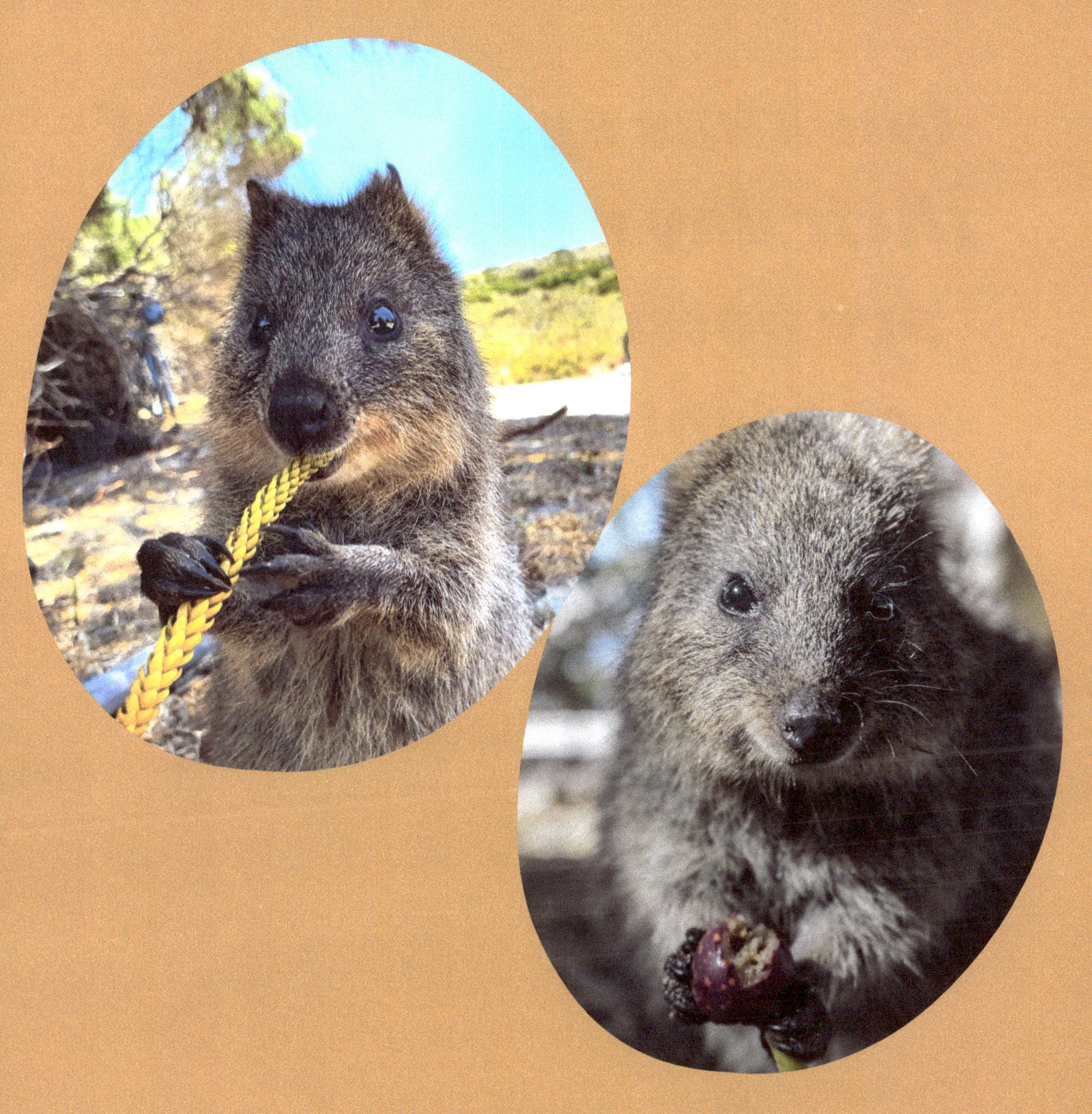

Quokkas spend most of their day napping. They are nocturnal, playing at night & sleeping in the day.

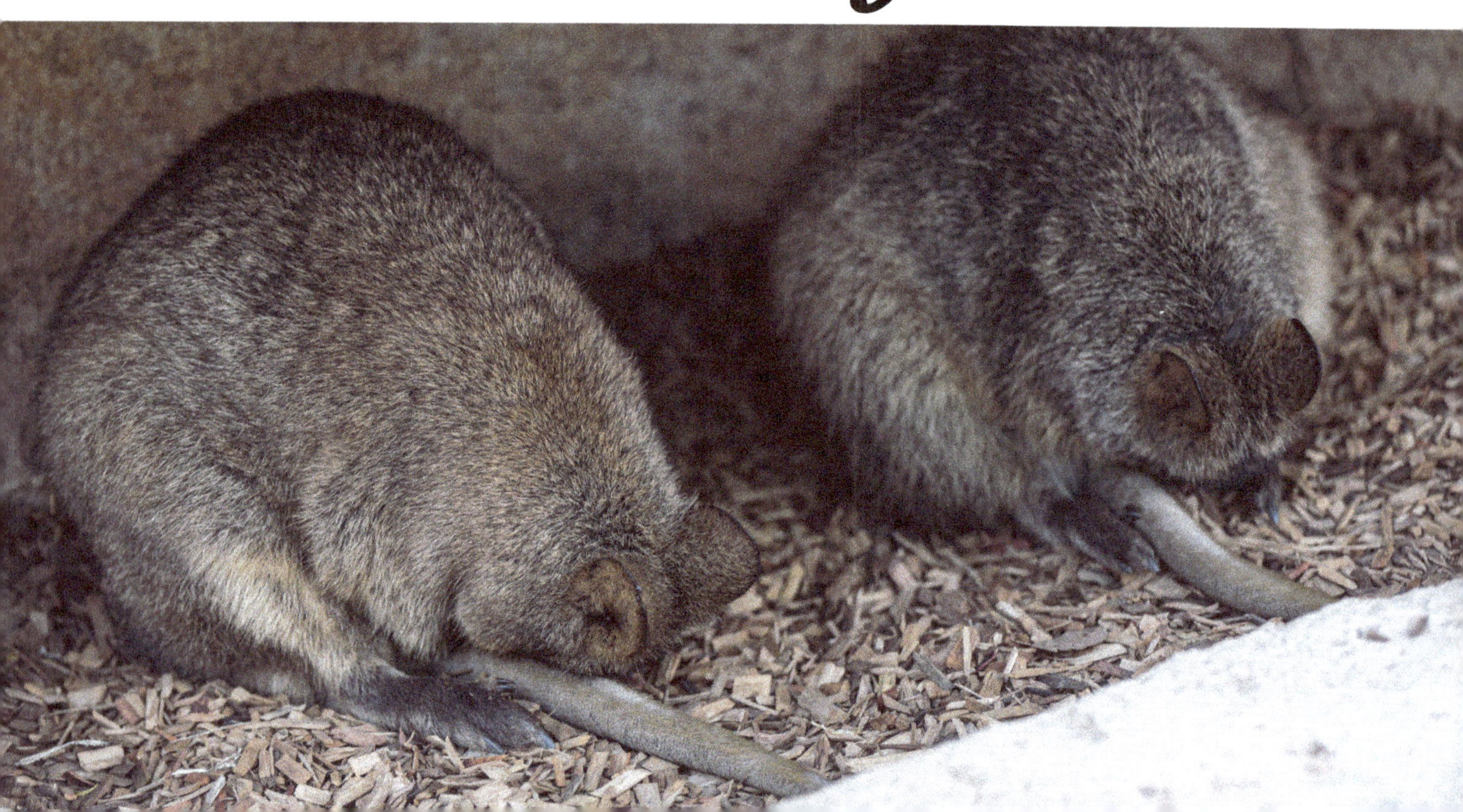

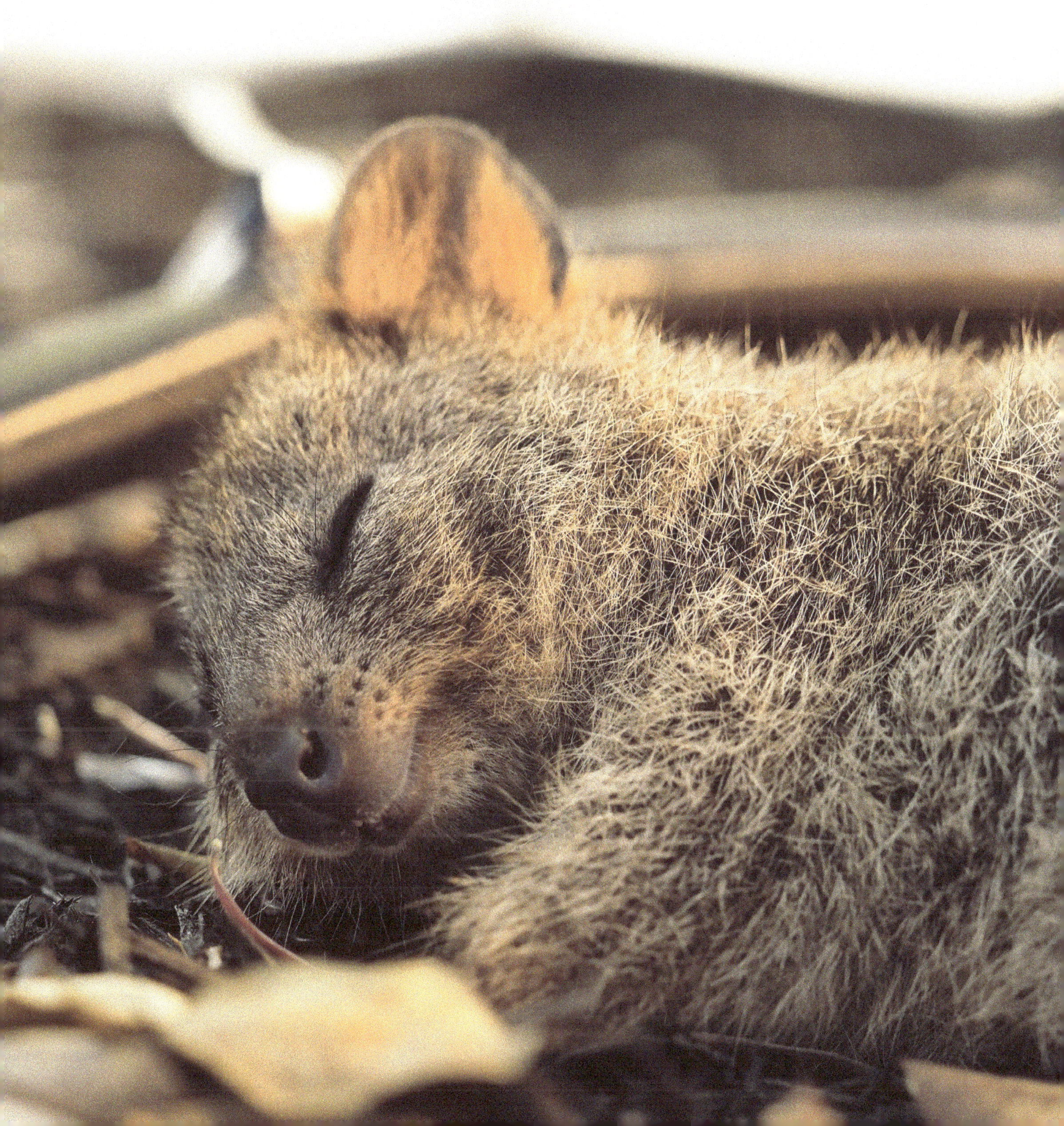

Quokkas may be small but the bring lots of joy into the world!

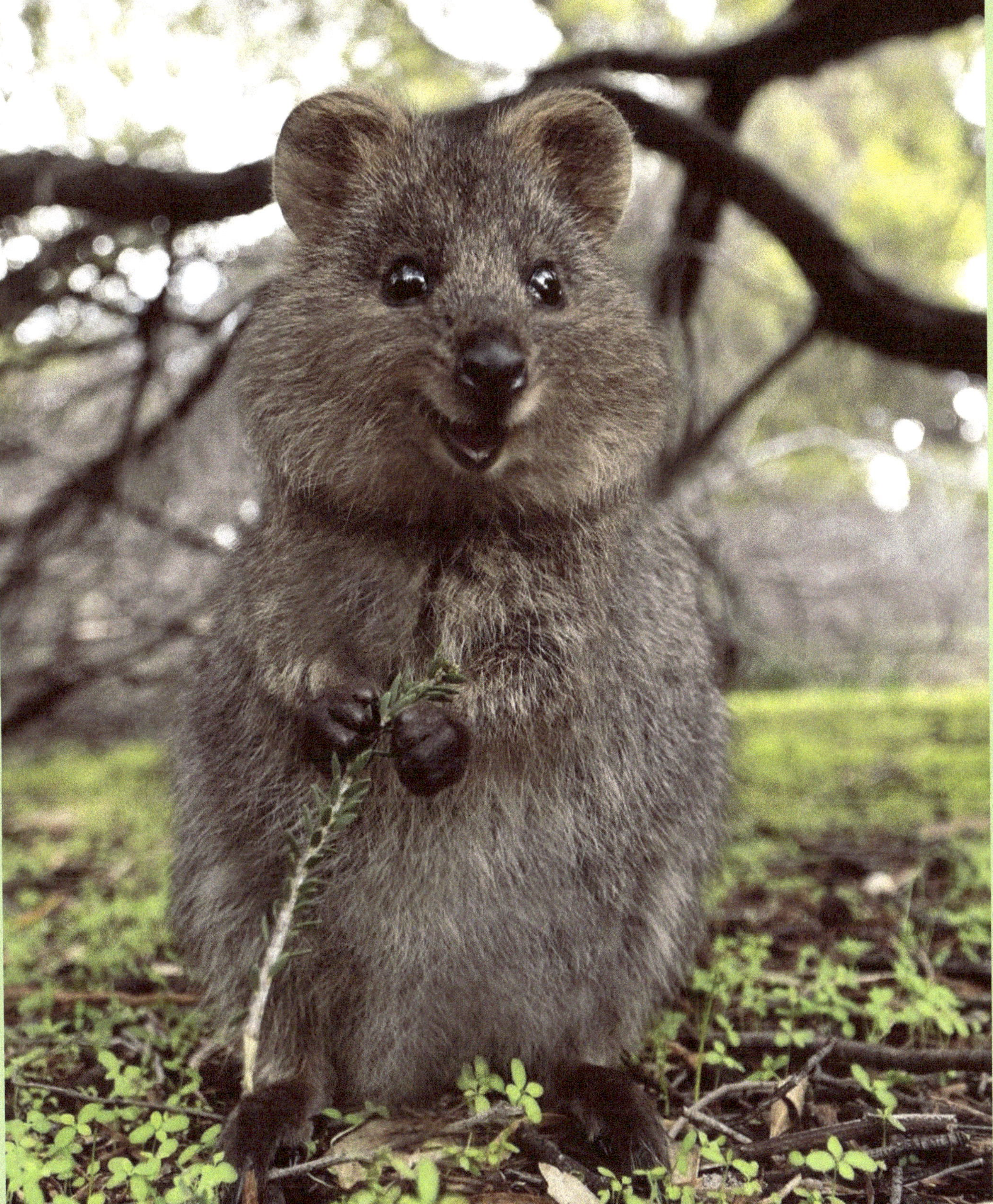

Quokka facts

- The quokka is also called short tailed wallaby.
- They are marsupials in the macropod (big foot) family.
- Quokkas are found on some smaller islands off the coast of Western Australia, particularly Rottnest Island just off Perth and Bald Island near Albany.
- There are thought to be 20,000 quokkas in the wild.
- Their primary threats are non-native animals like cats, dogs & foxes.
- Quokkas can also be observed at several zoos and wildlife parks around Australia, and The Saitama Children's Zoo in Japan.
- These iconic animals were first identified by Willem de Vlamingh in 1696 who mistakenly thought he spotted a giant rat.

Australia Resources

- Australia has more marsupial species than any other continent.
- It is the world's sixth largest country.
- Australia is the flattest, oldest, and most arid inhabited continent.
- Australia is home to many dangerous animals including some of the most venomous snakes in the world.
- Indigenous Australians have inhabited the continent for approximately 65,000 years.

Marsupials

- They give birth to relatively undeveloped young that often reside in a pouch located on their mothers' abdomen.
- Close to 70% of the 334 extant species occur in Australia.

Vulnerable Species

- There are currently 5196 animals and 6789 plants classified as vulnerable.
- A vulnerable species is a species which has been categorized by the International Union for Conservation of Nature that is threatened with extinction unless the circumstances that are threatening its survival and reproduction improve.

Thank you for reading this early science book with your child. Please take a moment & write an honest review of it on Amazon to help other parents & teachers.

If you liked this book, check out our other books about animals:

My First Owl Book &
My First Shark Book.

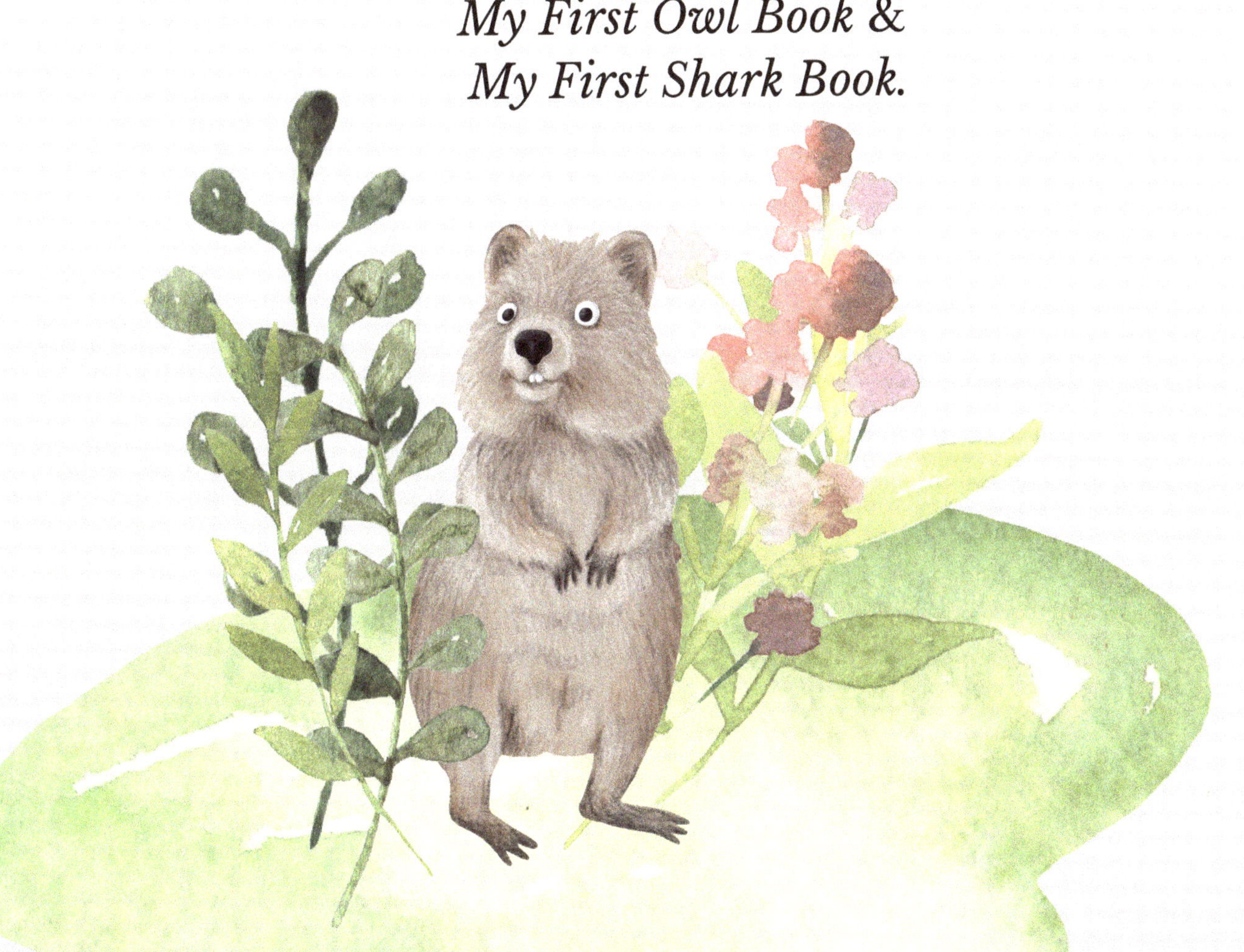